Anger Management

Control Anger & Stop Hurting

the One Person that Matters Most –

You

Addison Fenn

including specific information will be considered an illegal act irrespective of if it is done electronically or in print. This extends to creating a secondary or tertiary copy of the work or a recorded copy and is only allowed with an express written consent from the Publisher. All additional rights reserved.

The information in the following pages is broadly considered to be a truthful and accurate account of facts, and as such any inattention, use or misuse of the information in question by the reader will render any resulting actions solely under their purview. There are no scenarios in which the publisher or the original author of this work can be in any fashion deemed liable for any hardship or damages that may befall them after undertaking information described herein.

Additionally, the information in the following pages is intended only for informational purposes and should thus be thought of as universal. As befitting its nature, it is presented without assurance regarding its prolonged validity or interim quality. Trademarks that are mentioned are done without written consent and can in no way be considered an endorsement from the trademark holder.

Table of Contents

vi

Introduction

C ongratulations on purchasing this book, *Anger Management: Control Anger & Stop Hurting the One Person that Matters Most - You*, and taking the first step towards dealing with an issue that has no doubt been plaguing you for quite some time. Admitting that you have an issue with anger is a difficult step to take, but unfortunately, there are far more steps ahead of you if you hope to squash your anger issues once and for all.

To help you along your way, this book will provide you with everything you need to start your journey towards a life that is no longer defined by anger. First, you will learn all about anger and how this much maligned emotion really gets a bad rap. Next, you will learn all about the basics of anger management and how you can start preparing yourself for a more productive future today.

From there, you will then learn about the major flavors of anger as well as basic ways to counter each. For even more useful techniques, you will find chapters devoted to both the physical and mental tools you can use to help yourself deal with anger in an effective way. Finally, you will find additional tips that will help you mange your anger in the long-term.

Before you get started it is important to keep in mind that everyone experiences anger differently, which means the techniques that work in countering that anger are going to be different as well. All this is to say that if one or more of the techniques suggested in the following pages don't work for you, it is important to not get discouraged and to instead put your head down and keep trying different suggestions until you find one that sticks. The right solution for you is bound to be here somewhere; as long as you don't get discouraged, you will have a new and improved relationship with anger before you know it.

Chapter 1:
The Misunderstood Emotion

O
f all the emotions that a person can feel, anger is the one that can be the most difficult to pin down in the moment. There are times when you are angry that you feel as though you have never seen the world so clearly. As an emotion, you have no real control over when you feel anger but you do have control over how you respond to it, control that many people give up as an excuse to do something violent or dangerous and then not take responsibility for their actions after the fact.

Unfortunately, anger is often lumped in with violence and aggression, and those who have anger issues often make the mistake of writing it off without thinking about the many ways anger is a positive force as well. As such, the goal of this chapter is to shed some light on the most misunderstood emotion as the first step towards improving your relationship with it once and for all.

Anger has dimension

To many people, anger and aggression are one in the same, but this says more about the people who feel this way than it does about the emotion itself. Anger is actually far more varied than most people give it credit for. In fact, anger encompasses everything from the mild frustration a person might feel when they stub their toe all the way up to the all-consuming rage that they might feel when their pet is run over by a person on their smartphone.

While aggression often tags along with anger, it is its own distinct behavior that includes a very specific intention to do physical or verbal harm to a person or object. If you are currently dealing with anger issues of one type or another, it is important to understand the distinction as doing so is the first step towards taking back some of the power that you have no doubt given this emotion. Right now you may feel as though when you get angry the anger takes over, leaving you an unwilling participant in what comes next. This could not be further from the truth, however, and the rest of this book will show you how you can discover how to control the outcome of your actions or inactions.

Anger is predictable

Generally speaking, you can expect a person to become angry when faced with a situation that they see as either unfair or unpleasant. From there, they can be counted on to get even angrier if there is someone around whom they can blame for their predicament, or if it is clear the situation could have been prevented in the first place. If most people can be expected to react in the same way when presented with the same set of criteria, the question becomes why some people become so much angrier so much more often than others.

The answer is that everyone has a different threshold that indicates these criteria have been met. Those who have issues dealing with their anger have, for one reason or another, learned to take things to the extreme almost as soon as the option presents itself. For example, if someone cuts in front of you in line at the grocery store, you could either assume they did it on purpose, which is sure to cause anger, or you can assume they didn't see you and thus open the situation up to a host of additional possibilities.

Those who tend to lean towards the first assumption as opposed to the second may not even realize that there is a choice in the matter, which is why it can be so difficult for many people to come to terms with the fact that they have an anger problem in the first place. Once they come to an understanding that not everyone experiences anger in the same way they do, however, then additional progress can be made, but only if they are willing to work towards it. It is important to keep in mind that no change to something as major as the way anger is experienced can be completed overnight; this sort of thing can only come about with lots of hard work and dedication to success in the long-term.

There is nothing inherently wrong with anger

In the examples listed thus far, there is no reason to feel ashamed for feeling anger in the moment, as it is perfectly natural to feel angry when bad things happen to you that you didn't cause and that are out of your control. What's more, when anger helps people stand up to injustice or double down on their principals to create something better it can be a positive, productive emotion. No revolution was ever founded without anger and no innovation ever came about without someone first being angry at the status quo.

In fact, if you find yourself angry at something that you previously let pass without a second thought, then there is a good chance that your anger is a sign of personal growth, or at least that it can point out where personal growth is possible. If you find yourself growing angry at your current situation without understanding why, this can signify that it is time to take a closer look at the way your life is currently going to ensure that you are doing what you can to squeeze as much happiness from each day as possible.

Anger really is what you make of it, which means that it is up to each and every person to make the choice to express their anger in productive ways as opposed to giving in to the temptation to do something more destructive instead. When you feel a bout of anger coming on consider it a means of motivation, not a license to give in to basic instincts.

Unfortunately, for many people, the way they choose to express their anger often causes a variety of issues in their own lives and the lives of those around them. What's worse, the way they choose to express their anger actually ends up creating more anger in a vicious self-perpetuating cycle, as those who are the target of their anger begin to feel angry themselves.

When left unchecked anger is similar to cancer, in which it slowly infects every aspect of the angry person's life. It can cause them to lash out at their loved ones either verbally or phsyically, potentially leaving physical or mental scars that may never fully heal. While a brash young upstart might get away with getting angry at work at first, you can bet their career will stall when it becomes apparent that they can't contain their temper. Again, anger isn't responsible for all of these things but it is certainly the gateway to them, which is why it needs to be watched vigilantly to ensure that you always respond in a way that is beneficial for everyone involved.

Anger is more dangerous than you might think

While the worst case scenario for anger can be regularly seen on the news, there are far more insidious issues that it can take credit for as well. Known as maladaptive anger, this is the type of anger that leads to the destruction of one's personal property, substance abuse, or chronic verbal abuse.

It also leads to a wide variety of health issues, starting with undue strain on the heart. In fact, studies show that for two hours after you have a particularly angry episode your chance of having a heart attack doubles. This doesn't just mean incidents where you blow up and let your anger out in a verbal or physical way, as repressed anger can also contribute to heart disease. What this means is that while controlling your angry outbursts is a good place to start, in order to see true medical benefits from your new lifestyle you will ultimately need to learn to feel less angry in the first place.

In addition to putting extra strain on your heart, the two hours after a particularly angry outburst see an increased rate of stroke that is three times what it may normally be. For those who already have an aneurysm waiting in the wings, the risk of stroke increases to a whopping six times what it would otherwise be.

Beyond that, spending most of your time in an angry state actually weakens the immune system as your body is spending more time in a flight or fight state which requires additional energy, as opposed to in a relaxed state where it can prioritize general wellness. In fact, studies show that simply recalling a time when you were extremely angry can be enough to cause a dip in your antibody levels for upwards of six hours.

Chapter 2:
Understanding Anger
Management

Now that you have a somewhat clearer idea of what anger is all about, you can surely see why you may have had difficultly dealing with the issue head on. In fact, due to its complicated nature, there is a whole industry built around handling anger management in the best way possible. This is not to say that the only way to get your anger under control is in a professional setting, however, as you may do just as well, if not even better, with a personalized anger management plan that you create yourself. Much like anger itself, the right plan is going to be different for everyone and the only way you can know if you are on the right track is if you give it a try.

Anger management programs

Anger management programs typically provide a very clear set of recovery guidelines for the person dealing with anger issues. More importantly, however, it also provides those who choose to go this route a controlled space where they can release their emotions without worrying about backsliding into less productive behaviors. It also teaches participants constructive outlets for their anger rather than the destructive ones with which they are too often already familiar.

Frequently, this process will include a detailed discussion of the unique things that trigger each person's anger, with a broader goal of teaching everyone to be more aware of their emotions at all times and at every level of anger severity. The goal is for them to ultimately learn to use these signs as a roadmap to help control their anger.

This sort of controlled therapy environment isn't just for those who are dealing with anger issues directly; it is also for those who are dealing with the fallout of having spent too much time with those whose anger issues remain unresolved. This is because anger revolves in circles: As one person takes their anger out on another, they too will likely become angry. And as such, this perpetuates more anger in the world.

The goal of anger management therapy is not to cure anger, but to simply provide those who are dealing with anger issues as many different options to dealing with their issues as possible. Anger management therapy tries to change how one responds to negative emotions. This is because reacting with aggression removes any legitimacy you have for being upset in the first place. It can also make it easier to look at situations from alternate, increasingly productive, angles.

Anger management therapy is available in both one-on-one and group settings, though the one-on-one sessions typically contain a group component as well. Individual sessions will likely address specific facets of the patient's anger issues including things like work-related anger, relationship issues, or issues with family. If you don't manage to get your issues under control successfully on your own, and you allow your anger issues to grow out of control, then you may find yourself in a situation where you are ordered to attend one of these types of classes by the court as the result of domestic violence or other legal issues.

Unlike some types of therapy, anger management classes have no firm amount of time or classes required. Rather, it will be up to the patient and the therapist to determine what issues need to be worked on and when the classes are ultimately no longer needed. It is common for many anger management classes to provide homework assignments or tasks for participants to complete while taking part in the program. These are designed to strengthen the techniques and principals discussed in the main class and ensure that the participant doesn't backslide throughout the week. More importantly, however, they allow the participant to practice what they have learned in real world scenarios.

The National Anger Management Association provides anger management courses across the continental United States as well as online. It is the leading agency when it comes to dealing with anger issues and it certifies everyone from psychiatrists to religious leaders to life coaches interested in effectively seeking out and dealing with these types of anger issues.

Unfortunately, while anger management therapy works for many people, it isn't a magic bullet that is going to cure these issues overnight, especially if they are based on learned behaviors that have been around since childhood. In order to benefit from these types of classes, you need to be willing to put in the work on your end and really want to change. Without a desire to improve you will only end up running in place.

Creating your own anger management plan

If your anger issues are not that serious, or if you simply prefer working through things on your own, then there is no reason that you cannot create a personalized anger management plan and work through it on your own. If you are going to go down this route, however, then it is important that you are ready to do some research and some soul searching to start. You will need to have a clear understanding of what your triggers are, the various levels your anger may reach and the signs of each, and tools that seem to help you step back from acting on your anger in an unproductive way.

Getting started:

Depending on how much time and energy you have already put into learning about your personal experiences with anger, you may be able to provide all the required information or you may not know where to start. If you are starting from square one, then you are going to want to keep a journal of your angry experiences so that you can learn from them and discover the patterns that you tend to follow time and again.

In your journal, you are going to want to include every instance where you feel angry, no matter how mild or brief the experience might be. You will then want to rate the intensity of the anger, note the situation that set it off, list the outcome of the feeling, how you responded and what tools (if any) you used to calm yourself down. It is important to be extremely honest with yourself when you are taking these notes as the only way you will be able to improve successfully is if you have a quality baseline to work from.

Once you have a month's worth of data to look at, you can start picking out obvious trends to your anger that should allow you to determine your anger type as discussed in the next chapter. From there, you will be able to determine the sorts of techniques and exercises that are more likely to work in defusing future situations. It is important to not limit yourself when it comes to trying different means of dealing with your anger as you never know when you might come across something that will literally change your life forever.

In addition to staying calm and in control at all times, you are going to need to ensure that you are still meeting your needs while at the same time not infringing on the needs of others. Once you have a handful of techniques that seem to work for you, and you have managed to defuse a number of potentially angry situations without losing your cool, then you will be ready to formalize your plan.

Analyzing your results:

Once you have the basic outline of a plan that appears to work for you in mind, the next step is going to be to analyze the results and see where you can improve. This means keeping detailed notes in your journal, even when you feel as though you are starting to get the hang of things. This will allow you to consider what is working and what isn't and, more importantly, where the techniques you have in your arsenal appear to be letting you down.

It is important to not let yourself get locked into anything without trying plenty of options, and also to not lose hope if things don't appear to be proceeding as quickly as you may have hoped. It is perfectly natural for you to come across techniques that seem to work in practice, only to have them fall apart in a real world scenario. Similarly, something you never expected to work based on practice can happen to do the trick when it matters most.

When everything is said and done, it is perfectly possible for you to have a wide variety of different plans that are tailor-made for specific events or scenarios. There is no reason not to be as experimental and creative as possible, after all, if you try something new and fail then you are no worse off than you were to begin with. Additionally, you might end up with an entirely new coping mechanism that you would have never thought of otherwise.

Always have a goal in mind:

Once you have the basics of your management plan down, all that is left for you to do is to come up with additional goals to ensure that you don't end up resting on your laurels and opening yourself up to the possibility of backsliding further down the line. While these goals can be anything related to your anger issues that you feel is worth tackling, it is important to put some thought into your choice for the best result.

In order to determine if a goal is worth your time, you are going to want to ensure that it is SMART. A SMART goal is one that is specific, which means you can clearly tell if you are on track towards success or failure. A SMART goal is measurable, which means it has any number of clear steps you can take to reach success. A SMART goal is attainable. While a goal of becoming the mellowest person on the planet is admirable, it is likely not going to happen any time soon so you should aim a little lower. A SMART goal is relevant; goals that will affect your life in a positive way sooner than later are always easier to stick with. A SMART goal has a timeframe, which means you want to set a date for your goal that is achievable, but not so attainable that it makes you lazy. Stick with goals like these and you will have your anger licked in no time flat.

Chapter 3:
Know Your Anger Style(s)

While it is true that everyone is going to experience anger differently, there are still going to be a wide variety of overlap, perhaps more overlap than you might think. Broadly speaking, anger can be categorized based on 5 different expressions:

- The objective of the anger (punitive or restorative)

- The level of impulsivity the anger causes (uncontrolled or controlled)

- The overall mode of the anger (verbal or physical)

- The reaction the anger causes (resistant or retaliatory)

- The anger's direction (external or internal)

Additionally, it is important to keep in mind that your anger might primarily manifest itself in different ways depending on the situation you find yourself in, whether that feeling is frustration, or a feeling of being disrespected and/or threatened. Don't forget, anger is neither good nor bad inherently; its negative reputation stems from the type of anger that some people use to express themselves. As such, clarifying the type of anger you are experiencing is a crucial first step when it comes to controlling the expression of your anger and thus your reactions.

Assertive anger

Of all the types of anger, assertive anger is the most productive. Anger of this type often expresses itself by taking feelings of rage or frustration and using them as a means for positive change. Instead of avoiding confrontation or resorting to physical or emotional outbursts, this type of anger often causes those who experience it to get to work to personally change whatever it is that caused the anger in the first place.

This type of anger is often an extremely powerful motivating force and it can be used to overcome a variety of other emotions, including extreme fear. The biggest challenge with this type of anger comes in harnessing it properly and taking full advantage of its motivating force, before the anger cools and you learn to live with the status quo.

Behavioral anger

This type of anger is expressed primarily via physical means, and those physical expressions can be extremely violent. Those who experience this type of anger often feel overwhelmed by their emotions, causing them to lash out at whatever it is that is causing them to feel angry. When left unchecked this type of anger can lead to violent confrontations and can often lead to negative and unpredictable interpersonal or legal consequences.

When it comes to controlling this type of anger, the best thing that can be done in the moment is to give yourself some space from whatever the focus of your anger might be. This will give you an opportunity to regain control mentally and use any number of the tools described in the later chapters to prevent yourself from doing something that you will very likely regret. While there are more permanent options you can certainly work on to ensure that your anger doesn't build to these violent levels, this simple and effective option can save you from countless mistakes you'd rather not make. Once you have calmed down, you will likely find that you can reconsider the situation from a completely different angle.

Chronic anger

If behavioral anger boils up in the moment, then chronic anger festers like a bleeding wound. Specifically, it refers to a type of generalized resentment of other people, circumstances, events or even the self that can last for weeks, months and even years. It typically expresses itself via habitual irritation, which can have serious negative effects on a person's health and wellbeing.

One effective means of starting to deal with this type of anger specifically is to take an honest look at what it is that is making you so angry – not just on the surface but at its root causes. While it may take some time, getting to the root of your resentment will mean that you are able to leave your anger behind once and for all. This often comes in the form of forgiveness for some past transgression which can bring about extreme emotional catharsis.

Judgmental anger

This type of anger often masquerades as righteous indignation, though it often goes farther than righting a true injustice and can be triggered by something minor like a perceived slight, or what is perceived as another person's shortcoming. While this type of anger makes it easy to assume you have the moral high ground in the moment, odds are you are being just as offensive to another person through how you treat their personal opinions. Judging someone that you don't know or someone who hasn't done anything against you is the most common expression of judgmental anger.

While this type of anger can be difficult to deal with in the moment, the best way to ensure that it eventually becomes less of a problem is by making a conscious, continued effort to put yourself in other people's shoes. What' s more, you need to make a habit of not just doing it now and then, but really committing to the practice every time you feel your judgmental anger on the rise. Depending on how set in your angry ways you are, this might be an extremely difficult exercise to get the hang of at first, but if you persevere it will get easier each time you manage to do so successfully.

Overwhelming anger

This type of anger is one that everyone experiences from time to time, as it occurs when you find yourself in a rough situation that is beyond your control. It often brings with it comingled feelings of frustration and hopelessness. While it is normal to feel this way when you suddenly realize that you have taken on too much responsibility and that there is no way to change course, or when unexpected life events beat you down, this type of anger can become disruptive if you start to feel it over more insignificant events. Once that happens it starts to make it difficult for you to function normally.

The feelings of hopelessness that typically come with this type of anger can make it extremely difficult to deal with all on your own. As such, if you feel as though you are feeling this type of anger to an unrealistic degree then it is important that you seek professional help.

Passive-aggressive anger

This type of anger is primarily used as an avoidance technique, letting the user vent their anger behind a guise of normalcy. Those who resort to this type of anger on a regular basis tend to try and avoid any and all types of conflict and may even repress or deny what they are really feeling, even to themselves.

Passive-aggressive anger often expresses itself through things like sarcasm, thinly veiled mockery and pointed silences but also via behaviors such as chronic procrastination. Depending on the severity of the denial, some people experiencing this type of anger don't even realize that they are actually being aggressive, making it difficult to self-diagnose and potentially leading to less than ideal professional and personal outcomes.

While it may take a third party to alert you to your passive-aggressive behaviors, once you are aware of the issue the best way to start to approach the issue is through learning more healthy and assertive means of expressing yourself. This should allow you to develop your ability to articulate things that make you angry or frustrated in a more confidant and productive fashion.

If you find that you resort to passive-aggression because you are afraid of the potential consequences, then the best way to deal with this issue is to follow your fear down the rabbit hole and see where it leads. If you are afraid of confrontation when standing up for yourself in conversation, for example, follow this train of thought to its logical conclusion and consider why exactly you are afraid. Whatever the issue is, odds are it has nothing to do with speaking your mind directly. Try to take the focus off the expression of the issue and put it on the root cause where it can be addressed.

Retaliatory anger

This type of anger can be difficult for some people to control because it often happens at an instinctual level in response to a direct confrontation or personal attack, whether verbal or physical. Everyone has felt this type of anger at one time or another as it is also the anger that flares up when you want to seek revenge over a perceived slight whether real or imagined. Retaliatory anger can be especially useful if you are justified in feeling angry in what you have suffered through as it can motivate you to right the wrong in a purposeful and deliberate fashion.

While it can be useful when it comes to helping you take control of a poor situation, it can also lead to thoughts of retaliation which can be especially disastrous if the inciting incident was imagined or the other party was unaware of the issue. Those who are under its negative influence may often try to intimidate others and force them to come around to their way of thinking rather than talking things through.

In order to mange the negative side of this type of anger effectively it is important to make a point of taking extra time to think before you act in scenarios where you feel yourself starting to get angry. If you are already aware of this issue then the few seconds of extra thought should be enough to short circuit the retaliatory nature of this type of anger long enough for you to consider if what you are doing is justified. Generally speaking, by making a decision to diffuse the current conflict you will find that you are able to avoid creating a scenario where revenge is the only option.

Self-abusive anger

This type of anger causes the person feeling it to lash out at themselves for perceived feelings of shame, humiliation, unworthiness or hopelessness. It is a type of anger that is fueled by shame and is typically expressed by self-destructive behaviors like eating disorders, substance abuse, self-harm or negative self-talk. Depending on their personal predilections, some people may instead lash out at those around them as a means of masking their feelings of low self-worth.

Due to the warped view of the world that often comes along with this type of anger, once truly internalized, it can be difficult to diagnose yourself with this type of anger. If you do come to the realization that you are holding onto to self-abusive anger then a great way to start working through your issues is via cognitive refraining techniques such as those discussed in a later chapter.

Verbal anger

While this type of anger is considered by many to be less dangerous than the more physical types of behavioral anger, the truth of the matter is that it can be just as harmful, if not even more so, than its physical counterpart. The issue here is that verbal anger leads to verbal abuse and the psychological and emotional damage that is done can potentially stay with the victims for the *rest of their lives.* Verbal abuse can be something obvious like loud shouting and threats of violence or it can be more subtle and be expressed as harsh criticism, unfairly placed blame, or ridicule. This type of anger is more commonly expressed in relationships and families.

The easiest way to deal with this type of anger is to work to get into the habit of gating the things you say based on whether or not you believe they will hurt the other person. While, at first, you may be tempted to blurt out the first hurtful thing that comes to mind, eventually you will find that you are able to realize what you say is going to have an effect on the person to whom you are saying it to and edit yourself accordingly. Once you learn to control the impulse to lash out when you are angry you can learn to express yourself through assertive anger expression instead.

Volatile anger

This type of anger seems to appear almost out of nowhere, manifesting itself in those who seem calm one moment and furious the next, regardless if they are raging about a life altering event or the waiter bringing them the wrong order at lunch. If you experience volatile anger then you may calm down quickly but the destructive potential of your anger likely means that everyone around you feels as though they need to walk on eggshells or risk your temper blowing up in unpredictable ways. If left unresolved, this type of anger can intensify to the point where you could seriously end up hurting yourself or others.

One of the most effective means of combating this type of anger is learning the signs that you are about to experience a volatile episode so that you can cut it off at the pass. Once you can properly identify what's about to happen, you can then take whatever mental or physical relaxation techniques that you respond to and put them to work.

Chapter 4:
Tools to Treat the Physical
Aspects of Anger

Relaxation response

When stress floods the body in large quantities over a short period of time it triggers the body's flight or fight response. For those with anger issues either response may lead to feelings of anger. As such, if you fall into this category then you can likely short-circuit much of your anger by simply working on improving your relaxation response instead.

While you certainly won't be able to avoid every flight or fight response that gets in your way, by taking the time to learn how to enter a relaxation response at will, you should find that you are

43

able to control your angry outbursts far more reliably than may otherwise be the case. The relaxation state essentially puts the brakes on the flight or fight response, and thus anything that happens as a result, and forces your mind back into a state of complete equilibrium.

This isn't just a mental response either: Having a true relaxation response will increase the flow of blood to the brain, relax your muscles, stabilize your blood pressure, normalize your heart rate, and slow your breathing. Beyond these measurable physical effects, this exercise will also temporarily boost productivity and motivation, enhance your problem solving abilities and even temporarily improve focus and increase energy.

There is no one right way to achieve a true relaxation response, which means everyone has their own perfect way to practice entering this state. The one caveat to this is that passive activities like reading a book or watching television, while certainly relaxing, aren't actually enough to generate the physical effects of a true relaxation response. The right relaxation technique is going to be one that focuses your mind and interrupts your regular stream of thoughts enough to elicit the type of physical response you should be aiming for.

Generally speaking, those who find they become angry in response to common stressors will often find more pleasure from things that are going to strive to calm them down. This can be things like guided imagery meditation, deep breathing exercise, progressive muscle relaxation or mindfulness meditation.

Deep breathing exercises

The key to getting the most out of deep breathing exercises is to start each breath from the abdomen to ensure that you are drawing in as much air to your lungs as possible. This is an important step as breathing from the abdomen as opposed to the upper chest will ensure you are getting more oxygen into your system with each breath, a surefire way to tell your body that you are not as stressed out as it might think. In short, the more oxygen you get in short order, the less anxious, angry and tense you will feel.

In order to maximize your breathing, the first thing you will want to do is to sit in a comfortable position with your back straight. Once you are in position, you will then want to place one hand on your chest and the other on your stomach. Next, breathe through your nose, ensuring that the hand on your stomach rises while the hand on your chest does to a much less degree.

From there, you will want to exhale through your mouth, making a concentrated effort to push out as much air as you can while at the same time actively contracting your abdominal muscles. Repeat as needed.

Progressive muscle relaxation

This relaxation exercise is actually a two-step process in which you make a concentrated effort to tense and then relax various muscle groups in your body. Doing so tricks your body into assuming that you are not currently in the midst of a flight or fight scenario because all of your muscles are so relaxed – and nothing bad ever happens when you are relaxed. As an added bonus, it will help you become extremely familiar with the feeling of tension that is likely to precede an angry outburst, particularly what it will feel like in specific parts of the body. This, in turn, will make it easier for you to remain vigilant against your triggers so that you can take the right precautions as needed. Finally, this exercise can also be combined with deep breathing for maximal results.

Before you begin practicing this exercise it is important that you first consult a doctor if you have a history of back problems, muscle spasms or other similar injuries that you feel might be inflamed by undertaking it. To start, you will want to find a comfortable position to sit in; you will want to ensure your clothing is relatively loose and that you aren't wearing any shoes.

When you are ready, you will want to take a few deep, calming breaths to clear your mind before focusing all of your attention on your right foot. Focus on the muscles in your foot and squeeze them as tightly as you can. Once you cannot squeeze any more you will want to hold that position for 10 seconds. Next, you will want to relax your foot completely for another 10 seconds, considering the difference between the two states as you do so.

You will then want to repeat the same process with your left foot and then continue in the same fashion until you have worked your way completely up the body. While initially you will likely have trouble only tensing the muscles that you are focusing on, with practice you should be able to successfully isolate the target areas. Ideally, each time you perform this exercise you will want to do an entire circuit of your body including your feet, calves, thighs, buttocks, stomach, chest, back, arms, hands, shoulders, neck and face.

Mindfulness meditation

Despite having been a part of various religious practices around the world for more than two thousand years, mindfulness meditation never really caught on in the western world until the 1970s when a number of studies started turning up measurable health benefits – not just to the mental wellbeing of its practitioners, but their physical wellbeing as well.

This, in turn, led to a renewed interest in the practice and a new understanding of the many ways that being mindful can improve one's health by directly getting to the heart of many of the issues that are caused by anxiety in the first place. With the backing of scientific studies, mindfulness meditation is now being used in a wide variety of governmental institutions in the United States including prisons and hospitals.

Practicing mindfulness will help you have a better understanding of your thoughts as something separate from your actions while

Chapter 4: Tools to Treat the Physical Aspects of Anger

also helping you to calm your mind, two things of vital importance when looking to improve the way you deal with your anger. While initially, you will want to practice being mindful in a controlled environment where you know nothing is going to interrupt you, eventually you will be able to practice it virtually anywhere and at any time. This makes mindfulness a useful choice when you need something to distract yourself from the current situation long enough for the anger to pass.

In order to get started, you will want to find a comfortable, quiet place where you can sit for between 10 and 15 minutes. To begin, you will want to take a number of deep, slow breaths. As you do so, you will want to consider how the air feels as it enters and exits your lungs, the sound it makes and the tastes it brings with it. From there, you will want to expand this awareness until it encompasses the rest of your senses as well. Your body is always providing you with a wealth of sensory information; all you need to do is make yourself available to it and you will be flooded with more sensory information than you might expect.

Eventually, your goal should be to get to a place where your mind is essentially blank. In the short-term, however, focusing on sensory information is a great way to block out the steady stream of thoughts that are, quite likely, always running through your mind. This is where mindfulness, when used in the moment, can help with anger issues as when used properly it can disconnect you from whatever it is that you are currently angry about for long enough to calm yourself down. For more information, consider my book *Mindfulness for Beginners: How Present Living Can Change Your Life* where you can learn mindfulness techniques that you can use on the go.

Medication

As with many psychological issues, treating your anger issues with medication is possible. While the goal should ultimately be to be able to function without this particular crutch, while you are working on learning more long-term management techniques there are many different over-the-counter (OTC) medications that can help you tone things down a notch or two.

Antidepressants including Zoloft, Celexa and Prozac are all regularly prescribed to help with anger issues. While they do not target the emotion of anger, they have a general calming effect that can help with several types of anger. As with any other type of medication-based treatment plan, it is vital that you speak with your primary care physician about your options and about what may well work best for you. After all, the purpose of medication is to complement the healing process, not complicate it.

In addition to prescription medications, there are a number of supplements and other over-the-counter medications that are known to help with anger issues to varying degrees. These include chamomile, passionflower and Valerian Root, as well as Proloftin and Benadryl. These last two are anti-allergy medications that are known to reduce anxiety as well. Both chamomile and passionflower can be consumed in tea as well as in tablet form to help stabilize mood and reduce anxiety. Finally, if you live in a part of the country where medical or recreational marijuana is a viable option then that is known to stabilize mood as well.

Chapter 4: Tools to Treat the Physical Aspects of Anger

Chapter 5:
Tools to Treat the Mental
Aspects of Anger

Emotional intelligence

Emotional intelligence (EQ) is the measure of a person's ability to properly identify and manage their own emotions as well as the emotions of others. As such, depending on the type of anger you experience, you may find that it is extremely helpful not only when it comes to controlling your anger but understanding it clouds your thoughts and provides you with alternative means of communicating whatever it is that is bothering you.

Broadly speaking, there are four main pillars of EQ that you are going to need to focus on if you hope to use it to reign in your anger once and for all.

Pillar 1 – Self-awareness

Self-awareness is, without a doubt, the most important of all of the aspects of EQ as without it you can never hope to understand your anger, much less pinpoint the triggers that are the most likely to set it off. Without being able to look inward and determine if what you find is the best version of yourself it will be difficult to ever improve.

Pillar 2 – Self-regulation

Self-regulation is a natural extension of self-awareness as once you are fully able to understand what it is you are really experiencing, it becomes far easier to reign in problem areas that you may not have previously given much thought. Essentially, improving your self-regulation is going to allow you to understand what makes you angry and helps you prepare for situations where you believe you are going to encounter your triggers.

Self-regulation is all about thinking before you act, which is another byproduct of self-awareness as once you are more aware of your baseline mental state then it becomes far easier to notice when things are out of whack. While it will be difficult to back off from your desire to express your anger in negative ways, with practice you will find that it is far easier for you to walk back from that edge. Finally, improving your self-regulation will also make it easier to put yourself in the other party's shoes, which has the potential to diffuse the situation right off the bat all on its own.

Pillar 3 – Motivation

Those with a high EQ tend to be motivated because they understand the many ways that thoughts influence actions. If you want to improve your response to anger but feel as though you don't really have the motivation to follow through the best way to go about getting started is by setting personal goals that are far enough away that you have to work for them, but not so far away that they seem impossible.

Pillar 4 – Empathy

Empathy is another important component of EQ as understanding what others are feeling better you will not only be less inclined to subject them to your anger, you will often find that you can come upon a solution that doesn't leave you feeling angry at all. Improving your empathy will also make it easier for you to refrain from judging others, and even yourself. There is no secret to improving your empathy; all it takes is making an active effort to see where the other person is coming from. While you may not always be able to see eye-to-eye, if you open yourself up to the opportunity then you are going to be able to find some common ground with almost anyone.

Triggers

Improving your EQ by working on the four pillars alone will also make it much easier for you to pinpoint the triggers that cause you to lose your rational mind to your anger. Everyone has triggers, things that happen either externally or internally that drives out rational thought in favor of acting with instinct. Luckily, improving your self-awareness and self-restraint will not only make it easier for you to spot your triggers but it will also make it easier to change what happens when your trigger "buttons" are pushed.

Take responsibility for your actions

When you are first working to improve your emotional intelligence you are likely going to find yourself getting angry more than you should be, and it can be easy to give up responsibility for what's happening and blame your actions on anger exclusively. Luckily, improving your EQ should help you to understand that while anger is an emotion that flares up in ways you may not always be able to control, the way you respond to that anger is very much something that you have control over. You need to strive to control your reactions to anger in order to prevent yourself from being a detriment to you and others.

It is important to keep in mind, however, that just because you start to successfully get your emotions under control does not mean that you are always going to have a firm lock on them. Emotions are finicky things and there is no reason that just because you have a lock on your anger in one manifestation doesn't mean it won't bust loose in another unexpected way. When you do lose your temper, it is important to not feel like a failure and instead understand that it is a natural part of the process.

Improve your reactions

Once you have become relatively proficient at understanding when your anger is starting to get the better of you, the next logical step will be to track the reactions you have to it as well. The simple truth of the matter is that many of the things that make you angry make most other people angry to one degree or another as well. The difference comes in the way that you respond to the anger, and once you start recognizing common reactions that you experience you can start taking proactive steps to change those reactions for the better.

Keep in mind, improving your EQ is not about hiding from your emotions; it is about processing those emotions as effectively as possible as soon as you realize what is about to happen. Never forget anger in and of itself is not a negative emotion, but it is how you have learned to deal with anger that is less than ideal.

Cognitive Behavioral Therapy

Cognitive Behavioral Therapy (CBT) is a type of psychotherapy that analyzes the response you feel to presented stimuli and then asks why it is that you feel the way you do. As your anger issues are caused by irrational responses to commonly seen scenarios, CBT is effective as it offers patients an alternative path back to healthy, realistic thought.

Chapter 5: Tools to Treat the Mental Aspects of Anger

CBT operates on a few important principals, the first of which you should have no problem getting on board with: It is that the thoughts a person has will naturally influence both their actions and, over time, their behaviors as well. From there, it is all about changing thoughts to alter the actions that you take, both in the moment and eventually habitually as well. Therapists who practice CBT believe that everything is connected and nothing occurs in a vacuum.

The second important principal of CBT is that, from time to time, there are always going to be some things that happen that are legitimately beyond your control. Instead of obsessing over this immutable fact, CBT teaches that you should instead focus on the things that you can change as that is a far more productive use of everyone's time. This, in turn, will allow you to put your effort towards the things that will benefit you the most. Additionally, it is important to understand that actions, feelings and behaviors influence thoughts as much as thoughts influence behaviors, feelings and actions; which means that if you ever hope to truly be free of your anger you will need to break the cycle on all ends, not just when it comes to thinking peaceful thoughts.

Reinterpret the world around you

One of the primary things that keeps your brain busy all day is a constant struggle to make sense of all of the crazy things that are taking place around you at all times. CBT focuses on giving it new ways to interpret all of the data that you are constantly taking in at all times. No new thought ever occurs without passing through a filter of all your previous learned experiences. This means that if you ever want to break free of negative angry responses, you need to start from scratch by building a new response to common negative stimuli.

Unfortunately, this can be easier said than done. In order to deal with all of the information it is forced to process, the brain ensures that the actual processing power set aside to deal with thoughts is as streamlined as possible by running it through a filter of common thoughts, acts and experiences to determine if it is something you have seen or experienced before. If so, then the thought happens nearly automatically at an instinctual level. Currently, these thoughts are the reason that your default response is aggression or rage, but with lots of practice you can alter the way your brain thinks by default and insert new automatic thoughts in their place.

Keeping thoughts and emotions on track

As thoughts are almost always the cause of emotions, it is important to make an effort to not assume that everyone around you is always harboring some type of negative intention towards you. This one small change should go a long way towards keeping anger out of your default response list. After all, it is far more difficult to be truly angry at someone for an honest mistake then it is for a direct and personal slight. Then, with even more practice, you will find that you are able to replace the thoughts and actions that used to lead you to anger with more productive alternatives instead.

Assertiveness training

While you might feel as though those who are currently dealing with anger issues don't need any more help when it comes to asserting themselves, the fact of the matter is that assertiveness training can provide them with other means of asserting themselves that aren't so potentially harmful to everyone involved. After all, there is a difference between constantly being angry at everyone who stands in the way of your goal and using assertiveness to get what you want without alienating everyone else along the way.

This type of mental tool can be especially useful for those who deal with passive-aggressive anger as it gives them an alternative way to speak their minds without forcing them to step completely out of their comfort zones in order to do so. Perhaps unsurprisingly, true assertiveness has a lot in common with assertive anger in that it can be used to ensure that your rights are being respected and not being trampled by anyone else, either accidentally or on purpose. As such, if you find yourself easily hurt, betrayed, impatient, overly critical, or constantly annoyed with the world it may be a good idea to undergo assertiveness or personal boundary management training.

Chapter 6:
Dealing with Anger in
the Long Term

While your short-term goals should be all about managing any negative anger that you are currently dealing with, your long-term goals should be ensuring that when you do get angry it is a motivating force in your life, not something destructive. As such, once you have a personal anger management plan that works for you, your next goal should be letting go of any deep seated anger and just try to be happier in general. Happiness and anger are both emotions, and while it is possible to feel multiple emotions at once, which emotion do you want to ultimately lead your life?

Let it all go

If you are the type of person who has been dealing with anger issues for most of their life, then odds are you are holding onto old slights and grudges that can bring out your anger in an instant. As previously noted, old or imagined anger can be just as potent as anger over an event that is currently taking place which means that if you are ever going to truly live a life that is free of negative anger then you are going to need to make a conscious effort to let these memories go.

While this might seem easier said than done, this is because you have not yet made the decision to let the memories go, which lets them hang around compounding your anger over history with each new trip down memory lane. Do yourself a favor and think of the memory that causes you only a little anger, as it will be easier to start with. From there, work your way through the memory one last time, only instead of picturing it as vividly as possible, picture it as if it was recorded on an old VHS tape and the quality is extremely poor. As you watch, let the picture get fuzzier and fuzzier until it is indistinguishable from static. Then, picture taking the tape out of the VCR and placing it on a far shelf.

This visualization exercise can help you to put a cap on the memory and allow you to start building new mental pathways that don't involve returning to bad memories time and again. If you do find yourself thinking about it, simply picture yourself putting it back on the shelf and don't give it any additional thought. If you stay vigilant you will find that it is no longer nearly as relevant as it once was. You can then work your way up to more and more important memories as your familiarity with the technique grows.

Other more concrete techniques exist too for letting go of past events. I refer to these memories as "mental clutter", because all they do is fog your experiences and perceptions of reality. For more techniques, consider my book *Declutter: Free Your Mind from Mental Clutter*.

Verbalize your issues

For memories that are harder to shake, or for issues that you have caused because of your anger, you may find it especially cathartic to discuss the situation aloud with yourself or the person you wronged. You may want to write down your feelings or record them for an audio blog, whatever helps you really process what has happened. Understanding the true breadth of the situation using your greater knowledge of anger and how you can improve your responses should allow you to find closure in many cases.

While in some situations your anger may be largely justified, it is important to keep in mind that thinking in black and white only serves to increase the fuel that feeds anger in the first place. Even if another person wronged you initially, there are very few instances where one party is completely not at fault, especially if the event was serious enough that you are still holding onto it many years later.

Now it may be difficult to reopen old wounds in such an invasive manner, but it is vital that you power through if you ever want to get these issues off your chest once and for all. Never forget that your anger is only one part, an ever-decreasing part, of who you are. If you let it define you then you are giving it far more power than it deserves.

Don't be afraid to start small

After all the work you put in to getting to a point where you can focus on the long-term, know that small things that make you happy are equally important: Your general happiness can serve to keep anger at bay. It is no secret that anger gets in the way of love and happiness. Nevertheless, the simple truth is that making a concentrated effort to spend more time doing the things you love and taking care of yourself by eating right and getting enough sleep can make a huge difference when it comes to maintaining a generally positive attitude.

Exercise regularly

It's no secret that exercising releases serotonin into the brain which means you will feel happier overall. What's more, making exercise part of your regular routine will give you something new to focus on so that you don't suddenly feel at a loss as to what to do with yourself with your influx of free time – which you will have when you go from taking time to understand your anger and creating an anger management plan to actually implementing it.

The type of exercise that you pick up doesn't matter much: Committing to any sort of exercise will allow you to see results in a reasonable amount of time, which will encourage you to actually want to keep going with it. Not only will this ensure that your serotonin levels remain both high and stable, it will also keep giving you regular shots of positive reinforcement as all of your hard work starts to pay off in the form of real results.

What's more, this positive reinforcement should come with the positive results you are making day in and day out on your quest to conquer your anger. Tying something with more tangible results to the rather ephemeral nature of your quest to conquer your anger allows you to stack on your successes. As long as you keep up both conquests regularly you can think of your ever-improving body as the physical representation of all the hard work you are doing to improve your mental state.

Focus on the present

If you allowed your anger to get to a point where it enabled you to make serious mistakes then it can be easy to dwell on the past, regardless of what the present looks like. However, it is important to understand that if you stick with your anger management plan then you have come an extremely long way and no doubt took serious steps to distance yourself from the person you once were.

While it can be easy to dwell on the things in your life that you wish you could change, doing so will make it difficult for your mind to truly move on because you continue to invest yourself in the past. Instead, it is best to focus on all of the great things that you are currently doing to improve your life, and all of the things that you have to be grateful for. In fact, you should make a list every morning of the things you are most grateful for and carry it with you wherever you go. Then, if you feel yourself starting to return to your old ways, you can simply picture the things on your list and force yourself to think of everything that makes you happy instead. Over time, you will find the urge to be angry getting fainter and fainter.

In order to truly focus on the present or really consider the future, it is vital that you don't just lock your negative memories away; you need to also forgive *yourself* for the things that have happened in the past. While the degree of difficulty in this task will largely depend on the way your anger manifests itself, forgiveness is the only way you will be able to truly move forward. At the very least you need to be able to come to terms with the fact that if you had not done whatever it was that ultimately lead you to decide to take positive steps to improve your relationship with anger then you would not be the better person you are today. Don't forget, nothing happens in a vacuum: If a negative action ultimately leads to a greater positive response, then the negative action cannot be without some degree of merit.

Anger Management

Conclusion

Now that you have made it to the end of this book, *Anger Management: Control Anger & Stop Hurting the One Person that Matters Most - You*, you hopefully have a better understanding of the multifaceted nature of anger as well as your relationship with it.

While this book certainly includes plenty of tips to make your relationship with anger more positive, it is important to understand that anger is an emotion that will remain with you for the rest of your life. Far from a life sentence, it is important to remember the many things anger can do for you as well: If you are quick to anger over minor slights, then slights of injustice should be enough to get your blood boiling and help give you the drive to get out there and make a difference.

Anger Management

While it is certainly possible to get to a place where you can use your anger as a tool, it is important to understand that it is not something that is going to happen quickly. If you make the mistake of assuming that things are going to proceed at a rapid pace then you will only end up frustrated despite the fact that you are actually making a reasonable amount of progress. Instead of focusing on how far you have yet to go, focus on how far you've come and before you know it your rage will be a distant memory.

About the Author

Addison Fenn was born and raised in the city of Toronto, Ontario. While climbing the corporate ladder, Addison Fenn decided to move to the United States of America in search of better work opportunities. To maximize income so that more "clutter" can be purchased, Addison Fenn lived in one state for tax purposes while working in the neighboring state for higher wages.

Having come across the philosophy of minimalism, Addison Fenn dropped out of the consumerism rat-race to pursue the childhood dream of writing fantasy novels. Nowadays, Addison Fenn's life consists of freelance work, writing, and exploring the wonders of the great outdoors.

Made in the USA
San Bernardino, CA
04 July 2019